MAY   2017

The Deer on Mount Rainier

Anders Hanson

Consulting Editor, Diane Craig, M.A./Reading Specialist

ABDO
Publishing Company

Published by ABDO Publishing Company, 4940 Viking Drive, Edina, Minnesota 55435.

Printed in the United States.

Credits
Edited by: Pam Price
Curriculum Coordinator: Nancy Tuminelly
Cover and Interior Design and Production: Mighty Media
Photo and Illustration Credits: BananaStock Ltd., Brand X Pictures, Corbis Images, Digital Vision, Eyewire Images, Anders Hanson, Hemera, Image 100, Stockbyte

Library of Congress Cataloging-in-Publication Data

Hanson, Anders, 1980-
    The deer on Mount Rainier / Anders Hanson.
        p. cm. -- (Rhyme time)
    Includes index.
    ISBN 1-59197-784-3 (hardcover)
    ISBN 1-59197-890-4 (paperback)
    1. English language--Rhyme--Juvenile literature. I. Title. II. Rhyme time (ABDO Publishing Company)

    PE1517.H36 2004
    428.1'3--dc22
                                                                    2004047240

SandCastle™ books are created by a professional team of educators, reading specialists, and content developers around five essential components that include phonemic awareness, phonics, vocabulary, text comprehension, and fluency. All books are written, reviewed, and leveled for guided reading, early intervention reading, and Accelerated Reader® programs and designed for use in shared, guided, and independent reading and writing activities to support a balanced approach to literacy instruction.

Let Us Know

After reading the book, SandCastle would like you to tell us your stories about reading. What is your favorite page? Was there something hard that you needed help with? Share the ups and downs of learning to read. We want to hear from you! To get posted on the ABDO Publishing Company Web site, send us e-mail at:

sandcastle@abdopub.com

SandCastle Level: Fluent

Words that rhyme do not have to be spelled the same. These words rhyme with each other:

cheer   hear

clear   here

dear

peer

deer

sphere

ear

year

The goldfish bowl is clear.

When their team scores, Ralph and his teammates **cheer**.

Christina whispers a secret in Evelyn's **ear**.

The baby **deer** rests in a field of flowers.

When Shelly spilled her bowl of cereal, she said, "Oh dear!"

After his dad stopped the car, Nathan leaned forward and asked, "Are we finally **here**?"

Carl can **hear** his heart beat through the stethoscope.

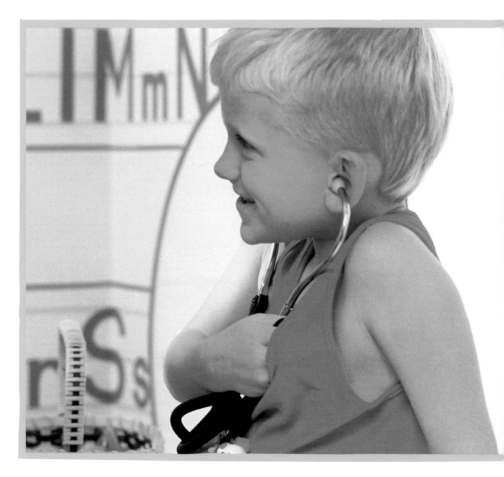

Courtney, Deb, and Mariah **peer** down through the spaces in the jungle gym.

Anne blows out the candles on her birthday cake.

She is turning nine this **year**.

Maxwell holds the soccer ball in the team picture.

A soccer ball is a **sphere**.

The Deer on Mount Rainier

14

It was my fear
that you'd never hear
the story of the deer mountaineer.

15

But it's certainly clear
that just last year
a deer climbed up Mount Rainier.

The weather was quite severe
and the drops were very sheer,
but the deer marched on with cheer.

At last the deer saw the summit appear.

He smiled from ear to ear.

19

The deer mountaineer
opened a new frontier.

He is really a true pioneer.

I'm being sincere,
so believe what you hear
when I report on the deer mountaineer.

21

Rhyming Riddle

What do you call a classmate who is a good friend?

Dear peer.

Glossary

frontier. the land at or beyond the edge of a settled area

peer. to look intently, curiously, or with difficulty; someone who is equal to another person in age, class, or rank

pioneer. one of the first to settle in an area

sheer. very steep

sphere. a round object, such as a basketball

stethoscope. a medical device used to listen to sounds inside the body

summit. the highest point

About SandCastle™

A professional team of educators, reading specialists, and content developers created the SandCastle™ series to support young readers as they develop reading skills and strategies and increase their general knowledge. The SandCastle™ series has four levels that correspond to early literacy development in young children. The levels are provided to help teachers and parents select the appropriate books for young readers.

Emerging Readers
(no flags)

Beginning Readers
(1 flag)

Transitional Readers
(2 flags)

Fluent Readers
(3 flags)

These levels are meant only as a guide. All levels are subject to change.

To see a complete list of SandCastle™ books and other nonfiction titles from ABDO Publishing Company, visit www.abdopub.com or contact us at:
4940 Viking Drive, Edina, Minnesota 55435 • 1-800-800-1312 • fax: 1-952-831-1632